30-Day

Writer's

Devotional

Jeri Darby

Jeri Darby
jeri@iamawriternow.com

ISBN: 978-1-958811-12-2
Printed in the United States of America

This Book is a Gift

For:

_____

"Thus says the Lord, the God of Israel: Write in a book
all the words
that I have spoken
to you.

Jeremiah 30:2

This book is dedicated:

to
Jesus Christ,
My Lord, Savior,
Author & Finisher
of
My faith...
&
The Writer in YOU!

Table of Contents

Table of Contents (Continued)

Introduction

Are you a beginning writer? Are you an experienced author? This devotional is written to both the beginning and seasoned writer. It is an inspirational jolt for overcoming challenges that may arise during your writing process. Look at it as a form of accountability. Let me be your accountability writing partner. Picture me whispering into your ear each day as you write—"you got this!"

Accountability may be the link you need to prevent fainting midway. It will give you a push towards completing your writing goal. I challenged myself over thirty days during live Facebook videos to complete my book. This project had been trampled and delayed by the trials of life.

Over thirty days I went live and my Facebook audience served as my accountability partners. (Videos available on Facebook and YouTube-I Am a Writer Now).

I was determined to regain the focus I needed to complete my book titled, "Say So! Open Your Mouth." It worked! I am the author of eight books and counting. I am a writing coach and have assisted numerous others to become authors.

My Facebook challenge kept me focused and I crossed the finish line on schedule. Listeners provided further support by pre-ordering my book. It was a great experience and I received positive reviews about the book released through this project.

Whether you are an aspiring or seasoned author, these brief devotionals will serve as a burst of fresh motivation to fuel your creative inclinations.

I embrace walking in my purpose as a writing coach. I am anointed to A-Activate, I-Inspire, and R-release the inner author inside others, who is desperate to escape! This book is the perfect gift for anyone engaged in the battles that *will* be encountered when writing a book!

Day 1

Start!

Where do I start? Where you start is not as important as—*starting.* Stuck? Start at the end. Write the end of your book, then go back and write the beginning. Start in the middle—it doesn't matter. Just *start!*

Once you begin, you can always go back and restructure. You may write the last sentence and discover—Hey! I shoulda put that at the beginning! I coulda added this or that! I don't need this! Do what you wish—it's your book!

Listen to your book, allow it to speak. It will direct and tell you where things belong. It will alert you when you are finished. Your book wants to be written.

**Just because you started off one way doesn't
mean the ending of the book has to be
the way you started.
Bernard Hopkins**

Day 2

Commitment

Commitment & focus are cousins. Make a sincere decision to follow God. Devote yourselves to learning, trusting, and obeying Him.

God released you onto the earth counting on your commitment to seek His wisdom to fulfill His plan for your life. Has He called you to write? Then Write!

Writing is the most important assignment in the world! Nothing happens in this world without words!

Yes, there are many distractions when writing. If you are committed to the process and place your trust in God, you *will* complete your book.

Commit your way to the LORD; trust in
Him and he will do this.
Psalms 37:5 NIV

4

Day 3

Tongue pen

Don't know what to write? What sets your heart aflame? What words pour from your lips with passion? What tragedies agonize your heart the most? What in God's creation takes your breath away? What inspired you today? Write about it!

What testimonies do you share over and over? What group of people fill you with compassion? What do others seek your assistance for? Write about these!

Are your words setting prisoners free? Have you overcome a difficult struggle? What is God speaking to you?

Listen to your speech— Allow words to flow from your lips through your fingers. Your tongue is a pen inscribing words upon the hearts of your listeners. Put it on paper!

The pen is the tongue of the mind.
Horace

Day 4

Two Sisters

An eighty-four-year-old woman with terminal health was referred to me. "I don't know why God has me still here. Maybe to finish my book," she gasped between breaths.

She completed and published her book. Later, she asked, "I found more poems. Can I add them to my book?"

"No, you will need to publish a new book." Terminal but determined, she completed another poetry book. She died shortly afterward while we were planning her book signing.

Reading her bio, I realized that I met her sister years ago in a writing group. She, too, desired to publish a book. Death claimed her beforehand.

**I must work the works of him that sent me,
while it is day, the night cometh,
when no man can work.
John 9:4 KJV**

Day 5

Time

Don't feel you have enough time to write? Don't bother troubling God with this complaint. Let me save you some time. This is what He told me.

"You have the same amount of time as men who walked on the moon, inventors, scientists, or any other person who has made world-changing contributions."

Seize the moment. Perhaps you can only manage small chunks of time; it's okay! Write—five, ten, fifteen, twenty minutes at a time. Day by day, little by little, you will get done.

You can waste time discussing and generating excuses, or you can invest time into writing.

For precept must be upon precept, precept upon precept; line upon line, line upon line; here a little, and there a little.
Isaiah 28:10

Day 6

Focus

Cell phone! I grab you to make one quick check... You distract me! I even forget what I intended to do. Hours later, I realize, "I've been robbed!" Time, I can never retrieve. "You focus thief!"

If technology hijacks your focus during writing sprints. Turn it off! You have voicemail, don't you? Sign out of Facebook! Writing is an act of war! Declare war on artificial Intelligence—*today!*

Take back your power! You are in control! *Focus, Focus, Focus...* Now write!

Focus is a matter of deciding what things you're *not* going to do.
John Carmack

Day 7

One Book Wonder?

" I am going to write fifty books!" "You should write one hundred!" Destiny, my granddaughter, was nine when she made this bold proclamation. *Hmmm*, it got me thinking.

"Why not?" New writers try to figure out how to cram their lives into a single book. Their message may become confusing; they may miss targeting their audience.

If you are like me, you desire to write about many things. You don't have to be a one-book wonder!

Let's look at other authors:

TD Jakes-372 +	Joyce Meyers-70+
James Patterson- 147+	Danielle Steele 185+

If God has given you more—write it!

May the LORD, the God of your fathers, increase you a thousand times over and bless you as He has promised.

Deuteronomy 1:11

Day 8

Story Call-outs!

It is not accidental that thoughts of writing the same stories haunt you over and over again! Your story is calling and pleading to be written.

Have you noticed that the same ideas keep invading your mind? Do you find the same thoughts scribbled in various notebooks over the years?

You can observe something over the course of your day that will later call out to be written. A lot is going on in our world. What may be unnoticeable to me may be screaming and demanding to be written—by you.

"Write, therefore, what you have seen, what is now and what will take place later."
Revelation 1:19 NIV

Day 9

Life Happens!

This book was birthed during my 30-day Facebook writing challenge. I imposed this challenge upon myself while completing my book titled, "Say So!" One day, I was a *no-show!*

Life happens! There *will* be no-show writing days. Your manuscript may get fidgety waiting, wondering, "Where is my writer?" It may start to feel nervous.

"Will I be thrust aside for months and forgotten like before?" Your story is anxious to be birthed and released!

Don't abandon your book and shatter the trust you worked so hard to gain. One no-show need not extend for days, weeks, months, or even years. *Life happens—get back to it!*

There is no greater agony than bearing
an untold story inside you.
Maya Angelou

Day 10

Creation Groans!

"Done with your book yet?" Not again, I thought, whenever someone asked. My book was on and off the shelf for over twenty years. I was embarrassed when questioned about it.

"That's creation groaning," God explained, people are calling forth the manifestation of what I have placed inside you." There are many levels of revelation hidden in this scripture.

Don't be embarrassed when others ask, "Where is the fruit of your vision?" God's creation is merely making a demand on the greatness within you. What God has implanted inside you has relevance. Not only to reveal His greatness to you but to impart a blessing unto others.

For all creation is waiting eagerly for that future day when God will reveal who his children really are.
Romans 8:19

Day 11

The Zone

I know this place! It's the zo-nnnnne! I wish I could stay here forever! This secret place is in hot pursuit by writers.

In this space, writing is obstacle-free. Words flow through you like a wide-open faucet of water. You realize, "My story is writing itself! It's the zone!"

Pages are filled with perfection, and little or no editing is required. The zone is a sacred place. I love it!

The more you learn to respect it, the more it will lead you into its revered chambers. Fully utilize these times of breakthrough. Seldom does a writer have the privilege of living there. But these rare visitations are priceless!

The one who believes in Me, as the Scripture has said, will have streams of living water flow from deep within him."
John 7:38

Day 12

Clarity

Whoa! I and my book are becoming one. I know what it wants to say before writing a word! I sense twists and turns before reaching them. I no longer attempt to manipulate it to migrate into other directions. True collaboration!

This place shows that you're listening to your book. You have earned its respect, and it is speaking to you.

This level of creativity is earned. It's a privilege granted to determined writers who persevere. It's your reward for not giving up. Embrace it.

> "It's a lack of clarity that creates chaos and frustration. Those emotions are poison to any living goal."
> Steve Maraboli

Day 13

Write it Down!

Words swarming in your head? Pick up the pen! Great ideas come and are quickly dismissed by the next one. You *think* you will remember—you probably won't! Distractions can siphon and remove things forever that we intended never to forget. Write it down!

Don't trust the treasury of thoughts parading through your head to instant recall. Commit them onto paper, a recording, or some other means of retrieval.

You cannot polish, shine, and decorate ideas and thoughts that vaporize into the abyss of the forgotten. Write them down!

You can always edit a bad page.
You can't edit a blank page.
Jodi Picoult

Day 14

Fresh Start

The zone has imprisoned me at times. I am held captive until the wee hours of the morning, exhausted, with my fingers dancing across my keyboard. Too often, I have fallen into bed drained, only to drag through the next day.

"Go to bed!" The Holy Spirit instructs. The more I tune in and follow His directives, the more effective my writing life becomes.

Arise and embrace His new mercies with a rested mind, ready to embark upon a fresh start! This practice has so enriched my writing life. Thank you, Holy Spirit!

The faithful love of the LORD never ends! His mercies never cease. Great is His faithfulness; His mercies begin afresh each morning. Lamentations 3:22

Day 15

Glory to Glory

The story of creation shares how God created the heavens and earth. Over six days. He took His concept from glory to glory. Each day, new splendor was displayed. On the seventh day, He rested.

Creation is a process. Outline the vision of what you hear God speaking. Surrender and allow Him to transform your story to reflect His perfect will. Full revelation is not unveiled all at once.

The Holy Spirit will add new dimensions to your book each day. God did not rush to complete everything in a day—neither should you. Allow new revelations of your project to unfold day by day, and remember, take time to rest.

And do not be conformed to this world, but be transformed by the renewing of your mind, that you may prove what *is* that good and acceptable and perfect will of God.
Romans 12:2

Day 16

Boxes

There are rules for everything, including writing a book. Many of them need to be adhered to. But don't allow yourself to be boxed in. Creativity cannot be contained within legalistic guidelines.

Go ahead—color outside the lines! You are finding your writing voice. Study, but don't be afraid to experiment.

Write about a purple cow or a red dog as others who allowed their creative energies to soar.

New ideologies and approaches spring forth in everything—including writing.

For I am about to do something new. See, I have already begun! Do you not see it?
Isaiah 43:19

Day 17

Excused Absence

Didn't show up yesterday to write? It's okay—don't beat yourself. Your book will forgive you. It knows the demands of life will cause times of separation.

It eagerly awaits to see if your time apart fueled fresh ideas, new approaches, and added dimensions to your story.

It's when you don't show up the next day, the next, or the next. Your sustained absences create distance. This break in intimacy demands trust to be re-established. Don't allow a few excused absences to cause you to generate excuses for future no-shows.

The one who believes in Me, as the Scripture has
said, will have streams of living water
flow from deep within him."
I Corinthians 15:58

Day 18

Forgiveness

Often your personal traumas filter their way into your story. That's okay because God wants us to declare His restorative power to others. But from a place of victory rather than as a victim.

Unforgiveness can be released in your writing and infuse your book with a spirit of rejection. When read, it will feed the spirit of rejection in others. This is not the end result God desires for your writing.

This does not serve God's purposes. Pray and allow the power of forgiveness to penetrate your heart so that your writing may release a healing balm.

And forgive us our debts, as we also have forgiven our debtors.
Matthew 6:12

Day 19

Birthing

Write your book over the weekend! In 30 Days! In 90 Days! There are wide options when choosing coaching offers. Yes, target dates for completion are important.

Just like an infant in the womb goes through developmental stages—so does your book. A story can be nurtured for years, nestled in the womb of your imagination.

Then yes, grab a midwife and push—it's delivery time! If this is a new concept, you could risk premature delivery of your project. It may be missing a few limbs. Be sure the vision for your book is full-term.

For I am about to do something new. See, I have already begun! Do you not see it?
Ecclesiastes 3:1

Day 20

Word Power

Nothing moves forward in this world without words. Nothing! It took words to create the universe. It takes words to keep it moving forward. Whatever your profession, whatever skills you have acquired, they were generated by someone's words.

Words expand us. We explode into new dimensions beyond anything we could have conceived—after ingesting words!

Take heed to what you write. Your words, whether spoken or written, are sown into the hearts of readers. They will produce a harvest of life or death. We shall give an account of the harvests produced in the lives of our readers.

A word fitly spoken is like apples of gold in settings of silver.
Proverbs 25:11

Day 21

Warfare

Writing is an act of war! The last thing satan wants is something released that will shed a favorable light upon God. We are God's witnesses. He is depending upon His writers to share stories of His mighty acts.

Once committed, you may notice a rapid succession of distractions hurled towards you. These come to snatch your focus whenever you sit at your laptop or pick up your pen.

These disruptions come in many forms. Attacks on family, finances, health, or other... When embarking upon your author's journey, put on the whole armor of God—intensify your prayer commitment. Write your book! God is with you!

Put on the whole armour of God, that ye may be able to stand against the wiles of the devil.
Ephesians 6:11

Day 22

Be Still

L istening. This is the most important part of the writing process. God seizes our times of stillness to speak. Otherwise, our minds zoom past thoughts that He wants to share.

Noticed that ideas come when washing dishes, driving, bathing, or trying to fall asleep? These are quiet times when God chooses to download fresh revelations for your book.

The same Holy Spirit who inspired the writing of the Bible is speaking to you. God sends fresh manna to ignite your story. Are you listening?

Sure, there are a lot of books in the world. But no one can write the book that God is dictating to you. Be still and listen.

"Be still, and know that I am God...
Psalm 46:10

Day 23

Next Time

You sit to resume writing your book. You wrestle with where to begin. Does this happen time and time again? It can be mind-boggling. Try walking away armed with a starting point for—next time.

"Where do I start?" This question can be forever put to rest by the strategy. This will also allow time for your thoughts to bathe in your imagination before writing.

You will reconnect with your book with a fresh resolve to produce quality writing. Try it today!

A person who doesn't have a structured way of writing their goals will experience disorder, even in the **comfort zone.**
Onyi Anyado

Day 24

Not Yet

I thought I was done with my book. I felt relieved and ready to publish! It was four am when I realized that I wasn't. A new chapter infiltrated my spirit and demanded to be included.

"When will I know when I am done?" Writers have questioned me.

"You will know," I reply while instructing them to trust the writing process. When your spirit has emptied itself of your project, you sense it.

Push! Then if nothing else comes forth—you're done. It's a great feeling!

It is finished!
John 19:30

Day 25

Prayer

Prayer is a mandatory part of birthing a book for Christian authors. The Holy Spirit is the first Author. He inspired the writing of the Bible. This book is the number one bestselling book in the world. It has been translated into more languages than any other book.

Partner with Him through prayer. Hire a writing coach if needed. They can provide a valuable service. The Holy Spirit is at your service free of charge. He provides fresh revelation and creative approaches as you write.

Invite him into each writing session by beginning with a word of prayer. Conclude in a prayer of thanksgiving for what God has imparted.

...Men ought always to pray, and not to faint.
Luke 18:1

Day 26

I AM Writing a Book!

You are a writer! You are writing a book! Talk about it! Sharing this with others makes you accountable. It fortifies the foundation of your author's identity.

Satan will *never* stop challenging your audacity to step into divine destiny as a writer. He hates you for it! Every time you pen a word, satan paces in fear of what part of his kingdom your words will destroy!

God has planted a book inside you! Release it! He has people waiting and in need of His words flowing through you. Let them know that your book is on the way!

**The Spirit of the Lord is upon me and
He has anointed me...
Isaiah 60:1**

Day 27

Pleasing God!

When a writer awakes to write, it brings Our Father, God, great pleasure! You did not just wake up one day and decide to write a book. It was ordained before the foundation of this world was laid.

Congratulations! You demolished every satanic effort to keep you stuck, muted, and confused.

Writing a book is not merely to gain a sense of accomplishment. It is a divine instruction.

Arm yourself with this perspective while writing your book. God has entrusted you with this assignment. Your "Yes" is pleasing to Him.

And whatever you do, in word or deed, do it all in the name of the Lord Jesus, giving thanks to God the Father through Him.
Colossians 3:17

Day 28

Now? or Later?

Let's face it, we are much more than writers. Some of us are working on creating multiple streams of income. We are wives, mothers, and employees, and some of us have clients of our own that we motivate and hold accountable.

All this while navigating an age filled with uncertainties and emotional unrest. Life's demands may cause you to keep lowering your writing goal until it no longer appears on your list.

Never allow what you do for others to overshadow your priorities.

If you cannot do it now—do it later. But by all means—do it! Keep writing first on your list of priorities.

"You always have time for things you put first."
Anonymous

Day 29

The End

The Bible says that God does the end, then the beginning. If you find yourself stuck somewhere in the middle—try it. Jump to the end and write your conclusion. Then, work your way back to fill in the gaps.

Many writers have shared that this has proven to be an effective strategy for them. I have found this useful in my writing and while coaching others.

The end of a matter is better than its beginning.
Ecclesiastes 7:8

Day 30

Don't Marry your draft!

What excitement! Typing that final period. It is finished! Your first inclination may be to mail, email, or hand-deliver it to the editor or publisher—right away. *Stop!*

If you have not self-edited your project—it's just a *draft*. I know you labored hard to deliver it. Your book is your baby—it deserves more. Make sure it is full-term, with five fingers and toes on each limb.

Check for complications that could result in sudden death! Hand over the best work you can possibly produce to the editor.

"That ye may prove what *is* that good, and acceptable, and perfect, will of God."
Romans 12:2

Prayer

God, thank you for placing the desire to write within me. I struggle to stay connected with this precious gift. Ignite the flames of passion that once consumed me. Clarify your plan and direction. Then give me the grace to follow.

Help me to hear and write under the inspiration of the Holy Spirit. Show me the audience that you have targeted for my story.

I desire to be your witness in greater measures. Help me to release even those things that I once thought would destroy me, if this is what you desire.

I pray others see your Gracious Hand upon my life and grasp the hope needed to hold on and call out to you for help. In Jesus Name,

Amen

Notes

What writing thoughts or ideas came to you while reading these devotionals?

_____

_____

_____

_____

_____

_____

_____

_____

_____

_____

_____

_____

_____

_____

My
Writing Declaration!

Starting today make

Your confession

I am a writer now!

_____

Signature

About the Author

Minister Jeri Darby is an author, speaker, and Writing Coach. She empowers writers to achieve their publishing dreams. Her Coaching services have stretched across the United States. Jeri is anointed to *activate, inspire,* and *release* the writer in others.

With twenty-five years of publishing experience, Jeri leaves writers equipped to write on a higher level.

Jeri offers online courses, author services, and more. She is the author of "Forgiveness, the Antidote" and other titles. Her goal is to author one hundred books.

Contact Jeri at jeri@iamawriternow.com or Phone 989 402-4721 to schedule a free consultation call.

A Tool to Get Started

Starting Points for New Writers
Is a Tool for writers.
It will complement this 30 Day
Writing Devotional.

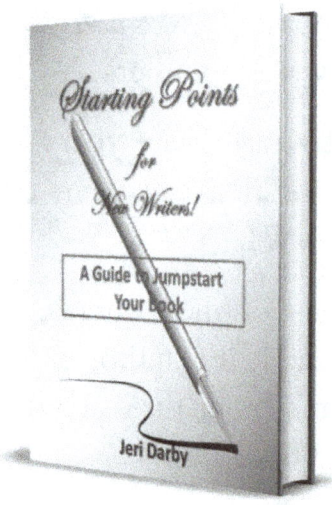

Recent Release

In a Snap! 28 Inspirational Stories of Answered Prayer

Other Titles by Jeri Darby

Available on Amazon

or

Website: www.iamawriternow.com

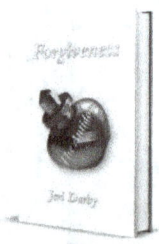  

Spanish

Spanish

Thank You for Reading
30-Day Writer's Devotional!

Watch for more new titles by
Jeri Darby this year…

Your Amazon and/or
Facebook Review

is appreciated!

The greatest way to support an
Author
Is to complete a review and/or
share your experience with
their book with others 😊

Blessings!

Need a Writing Coach?

Schedule your free consultation today!

Contact Information...

Jeri Darby

Visit My Online Bookstore at www.iamawriternow.com

jeri@iamawriternow.com

989 402-4721

Stepping Stones
Soar into Your Destiny!